PLANET PROTECTORS

Home Sweet Home

By Glen Phelan

Illustrated by Margaret Freed

PICTURE CREDITS

3-7, 60-64 (border montage) Corbis; 4 ©
Rachel Epstein/The Image Works; 5, 7, 61,
63 (border watering can) Getty Images; 5 ©
image100/Corbis; 60 © Kevin Morris/Getty
Images; 61 © Margaret Sidlosky; 62 © Frances
Roberts/Alamy; 64 © Tim Davis/Getty Images.

PUBLISHED BY THE NATIONAL
GEOGRAPHIC SOCIETY

Produced through the worldwide resources
of the National Geographic Society, John M.
Fahey, Jr., President and Chief Executive
Officer; Gilbert M. Grosvenor, Chairman of
the Board.

PREPARED BY NATIONAL GEOGRAPHIC
SCHOOL PUBLISHING

Sheron Long, Chief Executive Officer; Samuel
Gesumaria, President; Francis Downey Vice
President and Publisher; Richard Easby,
Editorial Manager; Anne M. Stone, Editor;
Margaret Sidlosky, Director of Design and
Illustrations; Jim Hiscott, Design Manager;
Cynthia Olson, Ruth Ann Thompson, Art
Directors; Matt Wascavage, Director of
Publishing Services; Lisa Pergolizzi,
Production Manager.

MANUFACTURING AND QUALITY CONTROL

Christopher A. Liedel, Chief Financial Officer;
Phillip L. Schlosser, Vice President; Clifton M.
Brown III, Director.

CONSULTANT

Mary Anne Wengel

BOOK DESIGN

Steve Curtis Design, Inc.

Published by the National Geographic Society
1145 17th Street N.W.
Washington, D.C. 20036-4688

Product #4U1005114
ISBN: 978-1-4263-5107-5

Printed in Mexico.

11 10 09 08 07
10 9 8 7 6 5 4 3 2 1

TABLE OF CONTENTS

Urban Neighborhoods

Many city neighborhoods across the country have vacant stores and houses. How did this happen? Where did the people go?

Through the 1800s American cities grew as factories were built. Factories meant jobs. Jobs drew people to live in the cities. This boom continued through World War II. In the 1950s middle-class people began leaving cities for suburbs. This urban flight is still happening today. But cities are trying to revive neighborhoods and make them good places to raise families.

Public Transportation

Most big cities provide public transport to help people to move around. People pay a fee to have a bus or train take them where they want to go.

Buses and trains travel along a set route. These routes cover all the places in the city. Some cities like Chicago and New York City have extensive train systems. Many people call this a subway system. In New York the subway is built in tunnels underground. In Chicago some of the trains travel on elevated tracks above the city streets.

Public transport is important to all cities. It connects people to their jobs, stores, and other places around town.

Meet the Characters

Miguel Ruiz

Miguel is a sixth grader. He likes to help his grandparents at their store. Other kids cannot understand why he likes to work there. But his grandparents help him appreciate his neighborhood.

Aleysia Ruiz

Aleysia is Miguel's younger sister. She likes to shop. But she may find that new stores are not always good things.

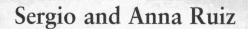

Sergio and Anna Ruiz

Sergio and Anna are Miguel's parents. Sergio works for the city. He helps the city plan where and how to build. Anna is a teacher.

Grandma and Grandpa Latoria

Grandma and Grandpa Latoria grew up in the neighborhood. They own a small store. They think the neighborhood can be even better than it used to be.

Lucy Landis

Lucy helps failing city neighborhoods. She talks to businesses and community leaders. Then she helps create a plan to save the area.

CHAPTER 1

A Changing Neighborhood

Miguel set the two canvas sacks of groceries down on the sidewalk. Quickly he turned up his collar and pulled the wool cap down over his ears. It didn't help much. When the blustery winds picked up, all he could do was turn away, close his eyes, and shiver.

"Cold enough for you?" said Miguel's Grandpa.

Miguel would have come back with a wisecrack of his own, but he was too cold to open his mouth. How Grandma and Grandpa were able to handle this winter weather so well, he had no idea.

Miguel Ruiz had spent the day at his grandparents' store. It was a small grocery store, mostly fruits and vegetables. Miguel often helped out—stocking shelves, putting out the produce, cleaning up in the back.

Some of Miguel's friends felt sorry for him. Seriously, who couldn't think of a hundred different things they'd rather do on a Saturday than work in a store? But

Miguel didn't mind. He enjoyed helping his grandparents. Besides, the store was a special place.

Grandma and Grandpa Latoria had started the business 40 years ago. It was a friendly neighborhood place; one of the few remaining "Ma-and-Pa shops" in this part of the city.

During warm weather, they set up fruit and vegetable stands out on the sidewalk. Children often stopped to buy fresh, crunchy apples for their school lunch bags. Mrs. Meale depended on Latoria's tasty tomatoes to make the best spaghetti sauce in town. And what store had the sweetest corn for Mr. Taylor's famous summertime barbecues? Latoria's, of course.

"How come your fruits and vegetables are always the best?" Miguel once asked Grandpa.

"We buy from local farmers whenever we can," Grandpa explained. "So the produce is always fresh. Plus, most of the farmers we buy from don't use pesticides. I think the produce tastes better when it's not sprayed with chemicals that you have to wash off."

"I agree completely," Miguel had said, biting into a juicy, green Granny Smith apple.

"It's getting harder and harder to buy locally, though. A lot of the farmers are being pressured to sell their land for housing developments as the suburbs grow. It's expensive to run a farm, especially without using pesticides—the amount of crops isn't as large. So when a good offer comes along, a lot of people sell."

That was too bad, Miguel thought. But it was a problem that seemed a million miles away. . . .

They continued their cold walk to Miguel's home. They passed a storefront window with a sign that advertised Al's Shoe Repair.

"Here's Al's place," announced Grandpa. "No one fixes shoes like Al."

Just then, a large man with a bushy mustache opened the door to the shoe shop.

"Hey, there he is!" bellowed Grandpa cheerfully. "Hi, Al. How's business?"

Al Pulaski locked the door behind him. "In a word, lousy," he grumbled. "People don't want to get things fixed anymore. If a sandal strap breaks, they just throw out the shoes and buy new ones. Broken buckle—throw 'em out. Worn out soles—throw 'em out. I can make them like new for a lot less money, but people are so quick to throw things away these days. I don't understand it."

"Are things really that bad?" asked Grandma.

Al looked down. "I may have to sell the business."

"Oh no!" Grandma was shocked. "After 35 years? That would be a shame. Maybe it's just a slow winter."

Al was in no mood for false hope.

"You know how it's been around here, Rosa.

Business has been going downhill for years. It's not like it was when we first started. Remember how lively this place used to be? There were so many people. They lived, worked, shopped, and played in the neighborhood. Everything you needed was right here."

"And you could walk everywhere," added Grandpa.

"Exactly," said Al. "I hardly see anyone walking anymore. In fact I hardly see anyone, period. Where did everybody go?"

"To the suburbs," Grandma proclaimed. They jumped in their SUVs and scattered."

"I love this neighborhood," said Grandpa. "But it does need a good shot in the arm."

"It sure needs something," said Al. "Well, have a good one." He waved goodbye and continued home.

Miguel felt bad that Al's business was failing. He made a mental note to check all of his shoes. If there was even a scuff mark, he was going to bring them to Al. But he knew that wouldn't be enough. Maybe if he got all his friends to do the same thing. . . .

Soon they came to a vacant lot.

"Hey, Miguel. My friends and I used to play baseball here. We'd cut the grass with our lawn mowers to make the field. Remember, Rosa?"

Grandma nodded as they stared at the lot. It must've looked a lot better back then, thought Miguel. Tufts of grass poked through the thin blanket of snow that covered the ground. A rusty, abandoned car stood among tall weeds the color of wheat. Empty cans, newspapers, and other garbage littered the place, either blown there or thrown there.

Grandpa wasn't noticing the garbage, though. He was picturing himself and his friends playing ball long ago. Miguel could tell by the faraway look in his eyes.

Miguel set down the groceries again. His gaze wandered from the lot to the building next door. It, too, was abandoned. Sheets of plywood covered most of the windows and doors.

The building had been this way since Miguel could remember. Whoever owned it didn't seem to care. It was like a lot of places in the neighborhood. Run down. Abandoned. Forgotten.

Miguel had passed this way hundreds of times before. But now, for the first time, he looked carefully at the building. He saw details he hadn't noticed before. The windows were arched. Some of the bricks of the walls formed a zig-zag pattern. The gutters were copper. They had turned bluish green over the years, like the Statue of Liberty in New York City.

"Isn't it a beautiful building, Miguel?" said Grandma. "It used to be a watch and clock factory, you know. A lot of people in the neighborhood used to work

there, including your Auntie Irene. It was such a nice place. Most people walked to work. Sometimes, they'd stop by the store."

"What happened?"

"The company moved out to the **suburbs.** To one of those big industrial parks."

"Does Auntie Irene still work there?"

"She did for a couple of years. But she didn't have a car . . . "

"Didn't have a car?" Miguel interrupted.

"That's right. She never needed one. Most places were in walking distance. If you were going downtown

suburbs – a community located just outside a town or city

or to another neighborhood, you took the bus or the rapid transit.

"Anyway, she got a ride with a friend who worked there. When her friend moved away, she was stuck. No buses or trains go out there. She bought a used car, but it took her an hour to drive each way. She decided it was too much time away from her family. So she found another job closer to home. It didn't pay as well, but they made do."

Miguel looked at the abandoned building again.

"Why doesn't someone fix it up?" he asked.

Grandma just shrugged.

Miguel remembered conversations he had heard in the store. Some people thought whole sections of the neighborhood should be bulldozed. "Tear it down and start again," they'd say.

That seemed like such a waste to Miguel.

"Grandpa, can we go?"

"Hmm? Oh, sure." Grandpa broke out of his dreamy thoughts. "But first I want to show you something. It's just around the corner."

"Fine," Miguel mumbled. Grandma and Grandpa smiled knowingly at one another. They held hands as they walked. Miguel trudged along, the sacks of groceries getting heavier with each step. This trip down memory lane was becoming a real pain.

CHAPTER 2

An Outrage

They turned the corner and walked down a short block. Miguel had never been down this street. At the end of the block stood a small, silvery, metal building. It reminded Miguel of an old-fashioned railroad car. A sign on top read Millie's Diner.

Grandma turned to Miguel. "This is where your grandpa and I first met 50 years ago. I was working here as a waitress. Your grandpa came in one day with his friends after a ball game. He sat at the counter and couldn't take his eyes off me."

Miguel started laughing. "Hey, Grandpa, was it love at first sight?"

But Grandpa wasn't paying attention. He was walking up to a large sign posted near the building. He read the sign out loud. "Public Hearing to be held February 4 at Lincoln High School. Will discuss proposed change of zoning laws to allow purchase and development of land by Shop-A-Lot, Inc."

A map showed the area for the superstore and its large parking lot.

"I can't believe it!" Grandpa roared. "That store's going to take up three whole blocks. All these homes and businesses, these big old trees—the diner! All gone?"

Then he looked closer at the map. "Rosa, look!" He pointed to a section of the map.

"That's our corner!" exclaimed Grandma. "Our store, our home, is going to be a parking lot?"

"Never!" boomed Grandpa. "This is outrageous!" With that, he stormed into Millie's Diner. Grandma and Miguel followed.

Grandpa went up to Teri, Millie's daughter, who now owned the diner.

"Teri, what's going on? What's that sign all about?"

"Don't you know? Didn't they talk to you last week?" replied Teri.

"Who? No, we were out of town last week. What's going on?" Grandpa demanded again.

Teri pulled a flyer from her apron pocket and handed it to Grandpa. It announced Shop-A-Lot's intention of buying land for the store. "Some people from Shop-A-Lot were going around the neighborhood last week, asking owners if they wanted to sell their property. They offered a good price."

"You're not going to sell, are you?" asked Grandpa.

Teri was wringing her hands. "I don't want to. Neither do a lot of others."

"But?"

"But, they said Shop-A-Lot will probably buy the land anyway, so we might as well take the offer."

"How can they buy if the owners don't want to sell?" asked Grandma. She was almost in tears.

Teri shrugged. "Apparently if a new development like a superstore will benefit the community, the City Council can let the developer buy the land, no matter what."

Now Grandma was getting angry. "They can't do that. They can't take our business, our home. And what

about all the other people?
A lot of them are elderly.
They've owned their
homes for years.
Where are they
supposed to go?"

Grandpa agreed.
"Heck, most of the
people couldn't afford
to move anyway.
Rents are much lower
here than in other parts
of town."

"So how can they say
the Shop-A-Lot will be good
for the community?" asked
Miguel.

"That's what I'd like to know," replied Grandpa.
"Teri, you may think this is a done deal, but it's not.
The public hearing is Thursday. It says in this flyer
that our councilwoman and a committee from the City
Council will be there. So will Shop-A-Lot."

"And so will we!" Grandma announced firmly.
"Come on. Let's get going!"

---

rent – a regular payment made to an owner of property for the right to live in or use that property

Grandma and Grandpa Latoria lived in the apartment above their store. Today, however, they were going to Miguel's house to spend Saturday evening with him, his parents, and his younger sister, Aleysia.

Aleysia came running out the side door.

"Miguel! Miguel! Tina and Carlos are here!"

"Oh, good. Here, grab one of these bags."

Aleysia snatched a sack of groceries, spilling two oranges that rolled down the freshly shoveled sidewalk.

She couldn't have been more excited. Tina and Carlos were her favorite cousins. They lived in one of the hundred suburbs that ringed the city.

Miguel greeted his cousins as he plopped the groceries on the kitchen table. "Hi, guys. How's life in the burbs?"

"Boring," replied Tina.

"Boring?" Aleysia was shocked. "How can you say that? You have that big, beautiful house and that big, beautiful park and that big, beautiful mall. I'd be at the mall every day if I could."

Miguel rolled his eyes. "Aleysia, I swear. Sometimes you can be such a dork."

Tina suppressed a giggle. She was kinder to her younger cousin. "The mall's okay, but if you've seen one, you've seen them all. I like the small stores around here better."

"Are you kidding? The suburban stores are awesome. I can find anything there."

"Yeah, but they're all chain stores. There's nothing special about them. Besides, you have to drive to get to them. In fact, you have to drive just about everywhere— school, library, dance class. You wouldn't believe the traffic. There are just too many cars. And my parents are always complaining about the price of gas these days. I think it's cool that you guys can walk to places like the grocery store."

Carlos perked up at the mention of groceries. "Hey, that reminds me. Is that bakery still around here? What's it called? . . . Keppers? . . . Kickers? . . ."

"Kepke's," said Miguel.

Carlos snapped his fingers. "Right, Kepke's. That place is terrific. The owner gave us a free butter cookie every time we went in. They're the best. Mom always says she can't find a decent bakery where we live."

"Yeah, well, you might not be able to find it here either," Miguel said as he put a bag of apples in a bowl. "It looks like it's going to be demolished."

"What?" said Carlos. "Why?"

"I'll tell you why," said Grandma as she stepped into the kitchen. She and Grandpa had been telling the adults in the living room about the Shop-A-Lot. Now she filled in the rest of the family.

Tina raised her hand to her mouth. "Oh no, Grandma Latoria, that's awful!"

But all Aleysia heard was 'Shop-A-Lot.' Her eyes widened. "That's a great store!" she blurted out. "We shopped there last year when we visited Tina and Carlos. You can get almost anything, and they have really low prices. I can hardly wait."

Grandma glared. "Aleysia, did you even hear me? Our home is in the path of that 'great' store. And a lot of other people are going to lose their homes and businesses. How would you like it if someone took your home away?"

Aleysia looked down. She started to sniffle. She realized what she had said. "I'm sorry, Grandma. I didn't mean it."

Grandma let out a deep breath. "Come here, Honey." She gave Aleysia a big hug.

"You can always live with us," Aleysia said between sniffles.

"I know, Aleysia. That would be nice. But that's not the point. Not everyone has a family they can move in with. Besides, we're not ready to give up the business that we worked so hard to build."

Suddenly a loud, shrill barking echoed throughout the house. "What's up with Mitzi?" asked Tina.

"I'll check." Aleysia dashed to the living room.

She found their dog standing on the back of the couch looking out the window.

"What are you barking at, Mitzi?" Alyesia looked out.

"Daddy's home!"

She ran to the side door to meet him. He set down his computer bag just in time to catch her as she flew into his arms.

"Daddy, Tina and Carlos are here."

"I see that. Hi, kids."

"How was the conference, dear?" asked his wife, Anna, as she gave him a hug.

"Excellent. We met with other urban planners from all around the world. You wouldn't believe all the great ideas people have for improving life in cities and reducing **pollution**."

"Well, I hope you have some ideas for our community," stated Grandma.

"What do you mean?" Sergio asked.

Anna explained about the Shop-A-Lot.

"Hmmm. I was wondering if they were going to go through with that."

"You mean you knew about it?" Grandma was starting to get agitated again. "You knew that we were going to lose our home?"

"What?" Sergio was stunned. "No. I knew the Shop-A-Lot people were talking with the City Council. But I thought they were going to use vacant land."

Anna showed him the flyer, which had a map. She pointed out where the new store would be.

"This is right in the middle of the neighborhood," Sergio declared.

"No kidding." Grandma was getting angrier by the minute. "We're not going to let this happen," she

---

pollution – materials that damage the environment and are harmful to health

vowed. "We're going to contact everyone we know. The City Council is in for a fight."

Carlos changed the subject as they sat down to dinner. "Uncle Sergio, how did you get home from the airport? I saw your car parked on the street outside."

"I took the train. The Orange Line from the airport to the Red Line to the Blue Line," said Sergio referring to some of the segments of the city's rapid transit system.

"I love the trains," Tina said excitedly. "We were riding next to one along the highway."

"Yeah, until it passed us," laughed Carlos.

"Traffic jam?" asked Miguel.

"Yeah, what else is new?" replied Tina. "It took 20 minutes to go two miles. In the meantime, three trains flew past us."

"Imagine how bad it would be if all the people on the trains drove instead," Grandma pointed out.

"Right," said Grandpa. "Now imagine how much better it would be if most of the drivers took the train."

"There would sure be a lot less traffic and pollution," said Carlos.

"I wish we had a rapid transit system in the suburbs," said Tina. Then her face brightened. "Hey, Uncle Sergio, can we take a ride on a train tomorrow?"

"Sure, the station is just a few blocks from here. At least, for now."

Miguel looked confused. "What do you mean, Dad?"

Sergio let out a long breath. "The City Council is planning on closing it. In fact, they might shut down the entire Blue Line."

Grandma dropped her fork. "Sergio, how can you let that happen?"

"Momma Latoria, I'm an urban planner, not a councilman. I don't have a vote on the City Council. It's all going to be discussed at Thursday's public hearing."

"Good. Then we can settle both of these issues. Eat up, everyone. We have work to do."

CHAPTER 3

Fighting Back

Saturday evening was supposed to be filled with card games, TV sports, and dessert from Kepke's. Instead, it was filled with plans, strategies, maps— and dessert from Kepke's.

"Clear the table," said Sergio.

Everyone lifted their plates of chocolate cake as Sergio unrolled a map on the kitchen table. It was a detailed map of the entire neighborhood. Lines showed the properties of individual homes and businesses.

"Cool map, Dad. Where did you get it?" asked Miguel.

"I have maps like this for every part of the city. We use them when we plan how to use the land."

"Enough chit-chat," Grandma ordered. "Let's get down to business."

Sergio smiled. "Yes, ma'am."

He used a felt tip pen to mark a large square on the laminated map.

"Okay. Here's where the Shop-A-Lot is supposed to go. Let's split up into teams and talk to each of the owners in this area. We can start going door-to-door tomorrow."

"What should we say?" asked Miguel.

"Tell people about the proposed store and the public hearing," said Grandpa. "See if they know about it."

"Let them know that we want as many people as possible to attend," said Grandma. "We want to make it clear to our councilwoman that we oppose this plan."

Miguel had an idea. "I think we should hand out a flyer. It could list the reasons we're against the store."

"Great idea, Miguel," said his dad. "People could bring the flyers with them to the hearing. It'll come in handy when we state our case. You and Grandma can work on the list tonight, okay?"

"We can tell kids at school about the hearing too," said Aleysia. "They can tell their parents."

"Great idea, Aleysia," said Miguel. "And I'll ask the principal if we can add the flyer to the parent newsletter."

Everyone got busy making phone calls, creating posters, and planning routes. It reminded Sergio of the headquarters of a political campaign.

Miguel and Grandma sat down at the computer to write the flyer.

"What shall we call it?" Grandma wondered.

"How about 'Save Our Community'?" suggested Miguel. "That's what we're trying to do, right?"

"Good thinking, Miguel. I'm glad you understand what's at stake."

The next day, the teams bundled up and hit the streets. Armed with determination and bagfuls of flyers, they headed toward the area where the Shop-A-Lot would be built. Miguel and Grandpa made up one of the teams.

SAVE OUR COMMUNITY!
ATTEND PUBLIC HEARING
THURSDAY, FEB. 4
LINCOLN HIGH SCHOOL

- Shop-A-Lot to replace homes and businesses
- Where will people go?
- How will superstore affect other businesses?
- Keep community culture for children and grandchildren
- City plans to shut down transit station
- Help keep the Blue Line open
- Let's improve our community together; bring your ideas

Their first assignment was a three-block stretch of houses and businesses along Rose Street. Millie's Diner stood at one end of it. Grandpa had no trouble convincing Teri, the owner, to attend the hearing. She was glad someone was leading the charge against the superstore.

That's how most of the people felt. Some, however, were happy to sell.

"I've had it with the crime and the crumbling streets around here," said one homeowner. "I'm taking the money and heading to the suburbs."

It was late in the morning when Miguel and Grandpa walked up to a house that had a ramp built in front.

"This must be for someone who's having trouble getting around," said Grandpa. "Maybe an elderly person in a wheelchair."

"No, that's Tom Evans's house. Tom goes to our school. He has **cerebral palsy**. He usually walks with leg braces, but sometimes he uses a wheelchair. Hey, there he is now. Hey, Tommy!"

Miguel ran to the side of the house. Tom Evans was coming down a small ramp from the side door. When he saw Miguel, he smiled. Then he leaned against his braces and waved.

cerebral palsy – a disorder that affects body movement. It causes muscles not to work correctly

Miguel was always impressed with how well Tom could get around with the braces. They looked terribly uncomfortable, but he never heard Tom complain. Still, he knew that Tom often felt sad about not being able to run and play like the other kids.

"Where you going, Tommy?"

"Just to mail a letter." He pulled a letter out of his coat pocket. "What's up?"

Miguel showed him the flyer and explained what they were trying to do.

"We're going to make this neighborhood the best place to live in the whole world."

"I know something that could improve it," Tom said. "What's that?"

"Fix all the old sidewalks. It's hard enough to walk in these braces. The broken concrete makes it really hard. I wish more buildings had ramps, too, like the school and library."

"Those are really great ideas. How about coming to the meeting on Thursday and telling people about them?" asked Miguel.

"I don't know. I don't really like to talk in front of people . . . but I'll think about it."

They walked with Tom to the mailbox. Grandpa saw that he had a hard time getting down the high curb.

"All these curbs should be sloped," said Grandpa.

"That's another thing you can bring up at the meeting, Tommy," said Miguel.

Tom walked home by himself. Suddenly, the crutch in his left hand gave way. He fell over into a pile of snow.

Tom's dad burst out of the house and ran up to him.

"Tommy, are you okay? Let me help you up."

As Tom struggled to his feet, he saw why he had fallen. His crutch had caught on the edge of a huge pockmark in the sidewalk.

"Dad, are you doing anything Thursday night?"

"No. Why?"

"There's a meeting I think we should go to."

CHAPTER 4

Grandma Hits a Home Run

"Wow, this place is packed!" Miguel exclaimed as they entered the Lincoln High School gym Volunteers were busy setting up more folding chairs. Grandpa chuckled.

"They were expecting only a handful of people. Boy, were they wrong."

Three long tables were set up at one end of the gym. Name cards identified the councilwoman as well as members of the City Council finance committee, the Rapid Transit Authority, and Shop-A-Lot.

"There's a lot of powerful people sitting at those tables," commented Sergio as he took his seat.

"Really?" responded Grandma. "I think there are a lot of powerful people sitting in all these chairs."

Miguel scanned the room. "There's Tom." He started to motion Tom to join them, but he saw that he was in his wheelchair near an open area. They waved to each other and Miguel gave him a thumbs-up.

The councilwoman welcomed everyone. Then she pointed to a map. "I'm sure you all know about the proposed Shop-A-Lot. It will be here, between Rose and Walnut Streets and 23rd and 26th Avenues."

The councilwoman spoke of her desire to improve the neighborhood. "This store will bring more people into the area and some badly needed tax money. Also, Shop-A-Lot will pay for new roads near the store."

Then people from Shop-A-Lot showed a drawing of the proposed superstore. Few were impressed. It looked like every other Shop-a-Lot, like a big box.

"The building of the store will provide about 200 **temporary** jobs," said one of the Shop-A-Lot people.

----

temporary – meant to last for a short time

"Local residents can apply for those jobs. The store itself will provide over 300 **permanent** jobs. Most of those will also be filled by local people."

The local people had lots of questions.

"How many jobs will be lost by the businesses that will be replaced?"

"What about the stores that will go out of business because they can't compete with Shop-A-Lot's prices?"

"How can I raise a family on the low wages and benefits from Shop-A-Lot?"

"I've lived here all my life. I'm not going to let you bulldoze my home."

No one sitting at the tables had good responses.

---

permanent – meant to last for a long time

Not every one was against the store, however. "I think Shop-A-Lot is a great idea," said one man. A few rude boos scattered throughout the room. "I say anything we can do to fix some of the roads around here is good. Besides, what's wrong with a nice, new store that sells things at low prices?"

A woman stood. "The big box stores should stay in the suburbs. We don't need them."

"Maybe this neighborhood could use a bit of suburban life," replied the man.

Another man stood. "There's enough pollution in the city without a parking lot full of cars coming and going all day. We should be trying to invite *people*, not cars."

"John, what do you want to do, go back to horse-and-buggy days?"

"Sure, if you'll clean up after the horses."

Laughter broke some of the tension in the room.

"Seriously, though. If we made our neighborhood more **pedestrian**-friendly and bike-friendly, that would improve it a lot. Then more people will want to live and work here. And we won't need Shop-A-Lot."

After hearing John's comments, Tom Evans looked more confident. He decided to speak. He told about his fall the other day and the difficulties of getting around.

---

pedestrian – a person who is walking

"I don't know if Shop-A-Lot will be good for the community or not. I'm glad that they'll fix some streets and sidewalks, but I'm not going to be living at Shop-A-Lot. I want to be able to go where I want to go, like everyone else. Our whole neighborhood needs improved sidewalks and entrances that are accessible to wheelchairs. That's one way to show that this community cares for the people who live here."

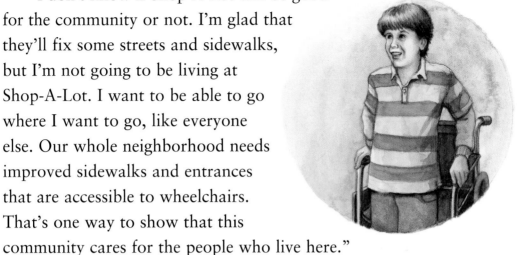

Everyone applauded. Tom smiled.

Next, the head of the Rapid Transit Authority spoke about the need to close the station and possibly the entire Blue Line. This caused a rumbling throughout the gym. Charts and graphs showed fewer riders and rising costs. "The Transit Authority simply can't afford to keep the line running," explained the director.

"I don't care what your charts say," said a resident. "My neighbors and I depend on the Blue Line to get to work, the doctor's office, stores, and other places. We always hear how wonderful it is to use public transportation. And then you pull a stunt like this?"

Another resident had a good point. "If we want to invite the people without bringing in cars, then we have to have trains and buses."

The people from Shop-A-Lot were also opposed to closing the Blue Line. They expected that many of their customers would use the rapid transit.

Finally, it was Grandma's turn to speak.

"When my husband and I started our store, the building was falling apart. Business was terrible. After a year, we were ready to quit and move out. But we loved our life here. We decided to stay, fix up the store, and make it a place that brings people together—people of all ages, cultures, and interests.

"Now, I know that fewer people are riding the Blue Line. I know the station is falling apart. And I understand that people have been moving away. But instead of closing the station, why not improve it? Make it a place where people want to go. Make it a place that brings people together. You may think you're doing that with Shop-A-Lot. I don't have anything against the store. I really don't. It's good for a lot of communities, but it's not what we need here.

"We can choose what kind of place we want to live in. We can make it the place that it used to be, even better. Let's build on the wonderful neighborhood we have, not wipe it out."

The gym erupted in applause. Grandma had hit a home run. But would her words help sway the City Council?

CHAPTER 5

K.I.N.D.

"Miguel, Aleysia, come here quick!" shouted Grandma. "They are talking about our neighborhood on the news. I think they are going to tell us how the City Council voted."

The news reporter on TV stood in front of City Hall. "As we reported to you last week, residents of the Winston Park neighborhood attended a public hearing to discuss the possible closing of the Blue Line.

"Well, today the City Council voted to keep the station and the line open, if a satisfactory plan can be presented to improve the area. That's a big 'if,' however. Winston Park has been in decline for years. Making it a lively, desirable community will be a hard task. Sergio Ruiz, an urban planner with the city, says the key to success is sustainable development."

The scene switched to Sergio.

"Sustainable development means developing an area to meet today's needs while protecting the needs of future generations. We want our community to be a great place to live and work, now and in the future."

"Sounds good, but how do you make that happen?" asked the reporter.

"Lots of ways. You use your resources wisely, whether it's money, energy, land, or buildings. You provide a mixture of buildings close together. That way people can work and shop close to where they live. They won't use up gasoline and pollute the air. You provide a safe and healthy environment. You make life fair by giving everyone the same opportunities for education and jobs. All these things make a community strong and vibrant."

The scene switched back to the news reporter. "Sounds like a tall order. We'll keep you posted. Meanwhile, the City Council has not yet voted on the proposed Shop-A-Lot issue that has Winston Park residents up in arms."

Grandma clicked off the TV.

Miguel smiled. "You did it, Grandma! I bet your speech last week saved the day."

"Thanks, Miguel, but nothing is saved yet. You heard the reporter. The City Council needs a plan that will work. I want to talk to your father about some ideas I've written down."

Miguel bolted from the chair. "I have a couple ideas too. I'm going to see what Arianna and Ben think."

Miguel talked with his two best friends for an hour. Then they went online to do some research. By the end of the evening, the kids felt certain they had come up with some good ways to help their neighborhood and keep the train station.

"Okay, so what do we do with our great ideas?" asked Arianna over the phone.

"Hmm . . . why don't we run them by Miss Paganini. I saw her at the hearing, so I know she's interested."

Miss Paganini, Miguel's science teacher, was more than interested. She had seen Sergio on the news and got an idea. She decided to start a club after school to learn about sustainable communities. Maybe the club could get involved in a local project.

Interest in the club was high. Twenty students showed up after school, including Tom Evans.

"Okay," said Miss Paganini. "What are some ideas for projects?"

Miguel raised his hand. "Arianna, Ben, and I were thinking of starting an organic garden."

"Great idea, Miguel. What made you think of that?"

"Well, I do a lot of gardening with my family. It's fun. And there's a vacant lot on Ridge Street. Maybe we can see if we can buy it and use it for the garden."

"Who's going to plant the garden?" asked Miss Paganini.

"We thought we'd divide the lot into plots," replied Ben. "Maybe 20 feet by 20 feet. Each class could be in charge of a plot. They will prepare the ground and then plant fruit, vegetables and flowers."

Excitement was building in the room.

"Can we sell what we grow?" asked Tom.

"Sure, that's the best part," said Arianna. "We figured we'd set up a vegetable stand at the station, like a farmer's market. I've seen one downtown in a plaza. At lunch time, all the office workers buy fresh veggies to take home."

"What will we do with the money?" asked a student.

"Whatever we want," replied another. "Why don't we just split it up among all of us in the club?"

"Is that the best way to use it?" asked Miss Paganini.

Miguel thought a moment. "Maybe we could use some of it to buy other vacant lots for other gardens. I've seen several around. How expensive are they?"

"I think most of those lots are owned by the city," said Miss Paganini. "I bet we could get them real cheap, maybe just a few hundred dollars each."

"Miss Paganini," Arianna called. "I think our club needs a name, and I think I have the perfect one."

"What is it?"

She went to the chalkboard and wrote K.I.N.D. (Kids Involved in Neighborhood Development).

Everyone agreed that it was the perfect name. Everyone but a student named Barry, that is.

"K.I.N.D.? Are you kidding? More like L.O.S.E.R. Lots of Stupid Environmental Rejects."

A couple of students tried to hide their giggles. Barry grinned. He was a class clown. He came to the meeting just to see what laughs he could get.

Most of the club members just glared at him. Without raising her voice, Miss Paganini said, "Barry, that was very clever. I hope you'll use your cleverness to come up with some ideas to improve the neighborhood."

He remained silent the rest of the period.

Fortunately, others did not. Once the ball got rolling, ideas flowed like water.

"Besides growing gardens in vacant lots, we can grow them on roofs," suggested Tom Evans.

Barry rolled his eyes.

"No, really," said Tom. "I've seen pictures of them in the newspaper. Lots of places in the city have them. They help keep the city cool in the summer."

"How?" asked Arianna.

"By replacing asphalt, for one thing. Most of the roofs around here are flat and covered with dark asphalt or tar paper to keep the rain out. The black roofs absorb the sunlight and get real hot. That makes the buildings and the whole neighborhood hotter."

"Yeah, I know how hot our asphalt driveway can get," said Arianna.

"Right. Anyway, plants also give off water through their leaves. When this water **evaporates,** it uses heat from the air. This cools the air and lowers the temperature. I read all about it in the newspaper."

Miss Paganini was impressed. "Sounds like a great idea. The more plants there are, the more they absorb, or take in, a gas called carbon dioxide. This way plants help to reduce the amount of this harmful gas.

Another idea was to make special bike lanes on the main streets.

"A lot of adults could use the bike lanes to ride their bikes to work," said Ben. "That'll mean fewer cars on the road, less noise, and less pollution."

The list of ideas grew. Miss Paganini could hardly keep up writing them on the board. It was clear that the days ahead were going to be busy.

---

evaporates – to turn from liquid into gas

CHAPTER 6

Helping Hands

While Miguel and his classmates were planning their projects, Grandma and Sergio were doing some organizing of their own, but not without help.

"Momma Latoria, I'd like you to meet Lucy Landis. Lucy is the director of New Day Development. They help communities like ours redevelop."

"I specialize in sustainable development," said Lucy. "Sergio told me about your ideas. I think they're terrific. I can help you with other plans, too. More than that, I can find ways to carry out the plans and get things done. We reach out to a variety of city agencies, banks, and community leaders."

Grandma was impressed. "Sounds like you're just the person we need. When can we get started?"

"How about right now? Let's go have a look at that train station."

Part of the train line was underground and part was above ground. In Winston Park, all the tracks were about 20 feet above the ground, supported by steel beams. The steel had been painted blue at one time. Or maybe it was orange. It was hard to tell. Very little of the color showed through the rust.

A train passed overhead as Grandma, Sergio, and Lucy walked under the tracks. A man stood near the stairs that went up to the train platform.

"Street Times. Get your Street Times here."

Street Times was a newspaper sold by people who were homeless. The newspaper cost a dollar. The seller kept 75 cents while 25 cents went back into publishing the paper. Some of the articles were written by and about the homeless.

"Hello, Franklin," said Grandma.

"Hi, Rosa. Heading downtown on the train today?"

"Not today. Did you hear the station might close?"

"Sure did. I wrote an article about it. The City Council is waiting for plans before deciding."

"That's what we're doing—coming up with plans," said Rosa. "It's going to take more than a new coat of paint on these old beams. I want to see this station surrounded by shops and restaurants. Most of the buildings are already here. Some have been empty for months. They just need to be fixed up."

"You know what else would help?" said Franklin. "An employment office. A lot of people hang around here with nothing to do. Some cause trouble. Most would

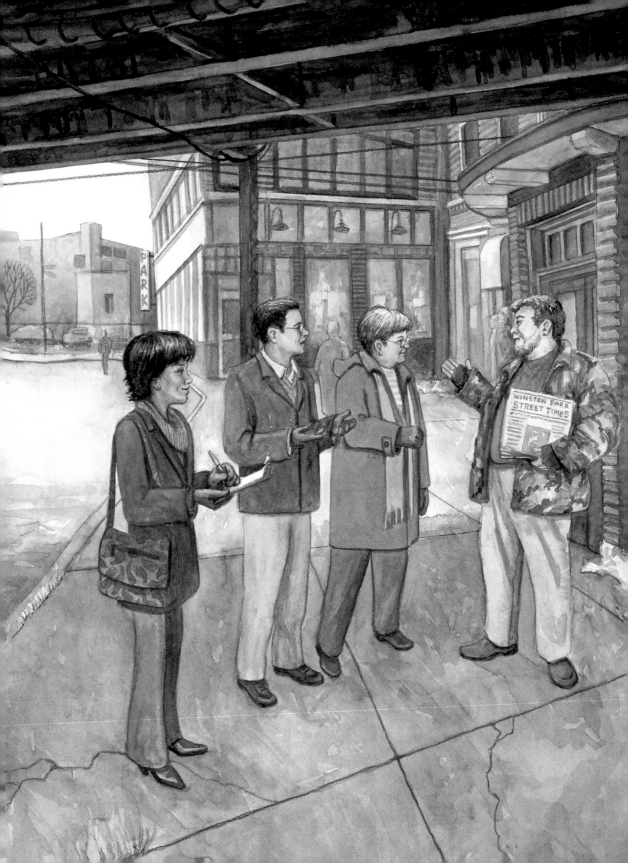

rather work, but they don't know how to get started."

"That's a great idea, Franklin," said Lucy. "I think doctor's offices would help too. We want this to be a place where people can meet all of their needs."

"Then how about a day-care center?" suggested Sergio. "Parents who take the trains could drop off their kids and pick them up right here."

"Now we're talking," said Grandma. "And I know a lot of people who would love to work at a place like that. Many of them are retired. They don't see their grandkids enough and would enjoy spending time with youngsters."

Sergio looked across the street. "Franklin, do you know what that lot is used for?" He pointed to a large corner lot. It was paved but most of the asphalt was broken and crumbled.

"The city used to park their Public Works trucks there. You know, dump trucks, street cleaners, things like that."

Sergio rubbed his chin. "I think that would be a great place for a plaza. Maybe a couple restaurants along the edge with outdoor seating. Maybe a fountain. The kids could also use it for their farmer's market. It's perfect."

"Yes," said Lucy excitedly. "And a skywalk could connect the station to the plaza. Then you wouldn't have to worry about traffic so much."

Grandma was thinking even bigger than that. "Forget the skywalk. Why not make this whole intersection just for pedestrians and bikes. Sergio, do you think traffic could be rerouted?"

"I don't see why not. I'll have to study the maps."

They talked about other ideas. Franklin took notes and said that he'd write an article about their plans.

Grandma was totally excited. For the first time in a long time, there was real hope for the community she cared about so much. But there was much more work to do. They headed to Lucy's office.

Meanwhile, K.I.N.D. was working hard on their projects. Once the word got out, teachers, students, and parents wanted to get involved.

Each class sent students to the K.I.N.D. meetings. Aleysia's class decided to build a butterfly garden next to the school. The class did research to find out what kinds of plants attract butterflies.

The eighth grade classes decided to put together a plan to improve the routes that kids take to school. A lot of the sidewalks were old and crumbly. Roots of large trees had even popped up whole sections of concrete.

"You know, our parents keep saying we should do more walking and bike riding to get exercise," said one student. "But I can barely ride my bike over all the bumps and holes in these sidewalks. And it's almost impossible to rollerblade on it. My uncle heard Tommy Evans talk about this at the public hearing. Why don't we get as many sidewalks fixed as we can?"

The students made a map showing which sidewalks needed fixing and where new sidewalks should be built. They also marked places that needed better lighting, stop signs, and crossing guards.

One day the club was meeting about the community garden. Pictures on poster board showed the different lots that K.I.N.D. was considering. The first one was the lot with the abandoned car.

Miguel ran the meeting. "Okay, so we've decided to have each grade take one plot. That leaves 20 plots for other people to use. Should we rent them or let people use them free?"

"We could rent them for a small fee, like $20 for the whole season. That could help us pay for supplies."

"But some people may not be able to afford even that. Why don't we set it up like a donation. We'll have a garden fund. If people can donate, fine. If they can't, they can still use the land."

"Okay, but if they sell vegetables at the farmer's market, I think a part of everyone's profits should go into the garden fund."

That sounded like a good plan.

Miguel went to other items on the agenda. "Lucy Landis, from New Day Development, is going to see about getting rid of that old car and cleaning up the lot. Then she'll talk to the City Park District about tilling the ground in the spring and providing topsoil.

"Angel's dad is going to build a tool shed for the garden. But we'll need tools to put in it. Here's a list of what we need."

Miguel handed out the list. It included rakes, hoes, clippers, gloves, and other garden equipment. Students signed up to go to hardware stores and garden centers for donations of materials.

"What about fertilizer?" asked Ben.

Miguel shook his head. "We're going to make these gardens organic. That means no chemical fertilizers. Instead, we'll try to fertilize with compost. We use it at home in our garden and it really works. My Grandpa is going to help us build a compost bin on the lot. It will hold grass clippings, leaves, and some food scraps like egg shells and coffee grounds. We'll mix it into the soil. It will help the plants grow."

"How about water?"

"I'm not sure. Maybe the city could put in pipes. Than we can hook up hoses."

"Why don't you use rainwater," came a voice from the doorway. It was a familiar voice, but Miguel thought he must be mistaken. He looked toward the door. Sure enough, it was Barry.

"Are you kidding?" asked Miguel.

Barry smiled. "No. Not this time. Haven't you ever seen all the water that gushes out of the downspouts when it rains? See that old building next to the lot?" Barry walked up and pointed to the photo on the poster. "You could get some sections of gutter and connect them to the downspouts to collect all the water. You could do the same with the house on the other side and behind the lot. You'd have barrels of water from every storm."

Barry drew a diagram on the board. He seemed to know what he was talking about. Miguel was shocked. He didn't know Barry was so good at building things or that he even cared about the project.

"So, do you want to be in charge of building a water delivery system?"

Barry shrugged. "Sure, why not?"

Maybe he really did care and just needed a chance to show it.

CHAPTER 7

Celebration

S oon it was time to present the community's plans at another public hearing. Lucy and Sergio had helped combine all the separate projects into one plan. She signed up architects who specialized in sustainable development.

One of the architects, along with Grandma, presented a plan for the new train station. It included all the things that Grandma and Franklin had discussed and more.

The doctors' offices, day-care center, and employment office were all inside a new building connected to the remodeled station. The building also included shops and restaurants.

"And here is the Volunteer Center," said Grandma proudly, pointing to the drawing of the plan. "People of all ages could go there to find out what groups need volunteers. High school students could be required to volunteer a certain number of hours before graduating. Students in grade school could earn gift certificates from local businesses, like the ice cream store that will be in the new station."

The plan also included new apartments and townhouses near the station. All the housing would be priced so that the people who worked in the shops and restaurants could buy or rent them.

"All of the buildings at the station will be built to save energy," the architect explained. "Solar panels on the roof will use the sun's energy to produce much of the electricity and hot water. Rooftop gardens will help keep the area cooler. They'll also absorb rainwater, which will reduce the amount of rainwater that runs off into the sewer system."

The lot across the street would become an outdoor plaza, like Sergio had suggested.

The architect continued. "Notice that we'll line the plaza with trees, shrubs, and flowers. In fact, we'll plant a lot more trees around the neighborhood. Besides being attractive and providing shade, plants absorb carbon dioxide, which is a major greenhouse gas. We're looking to improve the community in every possible way.

As you can see, one of the streets going by the station will be blocked off to traffic. In addition to the train, mini-buses running on natural gas will help people get around."

Heads were nodding in agreement throughout the gym. Many of the people at the front tables seemed impressed too.

Next, Lucy showed a plan for small houses to be built around the community. One of those places was on some of the land that Shop-A-Lot wanted to build on. The Shop-A-Lot people weren't too happy when they saw what Lucy had in mind. Some of the empty houses in the area would be bulldozed. Then the city would donate the land to the developer to build the new houses. They, too, would be energy efficient and use solar energy.

Lucy and Sergio were working to find people who wanted to improve or renovate some of the empty houses. They already had someone who was interested in the house next to the community garden.

It was an amazing plan. But most impressive were the projects that Miguel presented for K.I.N.D. In just a few short weeks, they had plans, maps, materials, and volunteers lined up.

The City Council was also impressed. The next day, they voted to deny Shop-A-Lot a building permit. Furthermore, they voted to keep the Blue Line and train station open. Latoria's was saved! So was Millie's Diner, Kepke's Bakery, and most other buildings in the neighborhood. One job was completed, but another lay ahead.

It was the busiest spring Winston Park had seen in years. Some buildings were being torn down. Others were being fixed up. The Blue Line was shut down—but only until the tracks were repaired or replaced. You could barely walk two blocks without running into construction. No one was complaining, though.

The community garden was a beehive of activity too. Not every shop owner could donate materials, but many of them donated something more precious—their time and expertise. Grandpa was doing his best to supervise.

Every evening, people gathered in their front yards and on the sidewalks. There were lots of new faces.

TV stations and newspapers ran stories about the community, and it was becoming a popular place to live.

One evening, Miguel and his family walked over to Millie's Diner. Teri had invited them for a special dinner.

Before eating, they all raised their glasses in a toast. After Teri thanked everyone, Grandma rose to speak.

"Henry and I first met here 50 years ago. It's more than a restaurant. It brings people together. May it remain so for another 50 years."

The sun was setting as they finished dessert. Then one of Miguel's friends came rushing into the diner.

"Hey, Miguel. We're getting people together for a soccer game. Are you in?"

"Mom, can I go?"

"All right but just for an hour."

He rushed toward the door. As he did, he accidentally knocked a backpack that was flung over the back of a chair.

"Oh, I'm sorry." He bent down to pick it up just as the girl sitting there did the same. They almost konked heads. Miguel picked up the backpack and strapped it over her chair.

"I'm . . ." He was going to apologize again, but couldn't find the words. He just stared with a goofy grin on his face.

"Miguel, come on," called his friend.

The girl smiled back. "Thanks for picking up my pack. My name his Laura."

Miguel finally spoke. "Hi, I'm Miguel."

"Do you live around here?"

"Yes. A few blocks away."

"We just moved in. Maybe I'll see you around."

Miguel nodded. "I hope so."

Grandma and Grandpa were watching. Grandpa turned to his wife, smiled, and winked. He was thinking about a special moment 50 years ago, all the special moments that followed, and all the special moments to come.

Community Garden

Community gardens are one way people are trying to strengthen pride in neighborhoods. Abandoned property, parks, and even parking lots are all opportunities for gardens. Gardens make neighborhoods look cared for. They even help residents save money on grocery bills.

Some gardens can be planted right away. Other times the soil is unhealthy. When that happens, gardens can be made in pots or in raised beds. Raised beds are gardens built on top of the ground.

Some cities are even encouraging people to build gardens on roofs! With creativity, all city dwellers can have gardens—and healthier neighborhoods.

Urban Renewal

Urban renewal might sound like a complex idea. But it's simple if you break it down. *Urban* relates to cities. *Renew* means to start over. So urban renewal is like breathing new life into cities.

People are trying to renew cities in many ways. Sometimes businesses and homeowners can pay less taxes if they move to cities. Building new libraries or restoring parks can also help.

Urban renewal can also have a downside. As neighborhoods get nicer, rent and home prices can go up. High prices can drive out residents who can't afford them. Doing what's best for a city is a balancing act.

Sustainable Development

The story talks about sustainable development. This means building a city in ways that help people and the environment. How are cities doing this? People will not stay in a city that does not offer what they need. Good jobs and health care help keep people in neighborhoods. Transportation helps too. If people have their needs met, then they are more likely to stay.

No one wants to live in a polluted neighborhood. Protecting the environment is another way to keep people in cities. Some cities, like Chicago, are encouraging the building of "green" houses. These houses use less energy. They are built from materials that don't hurt the environment.

Sustainable development creates cities that people can, and want, to live in. This means providing jobs, parks, stores, clean air and water.

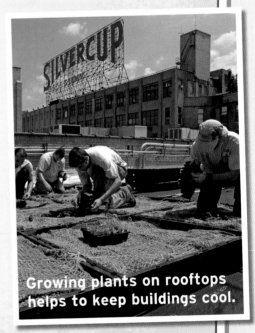

Growing plants on rooftops helps to keep buildings cool.

Write About Your Community

Think about your community. Is it rural, suburban, or urban? What makes it special for you? Write a paragraph about one thing in your community that should be preserved or kept.

- Make a list of things you like about your community that make it special.

- Pick one topic from your list to write about.

- Research the topic at the library or online. If you can't find information, ask older people in your community. They may know your topic's history.

- Write a paragraph about the thing you have chosen that makes your community special. Be sure to say why it should be preserved.

Read More About Protecting the Earth

Find and read more books about how people try to meet their needs while protecting the environment. As you read, think about these questions. They will help you understand more about the topic.

- How do cities help the environment?

- How do cities harm the environment?

- What can people in cities do to help stop global warming?

- What can people do to help protect our natural resources?

SUGGESTED READING
Reading Expeditions
Science Issues Today:
Global Warming

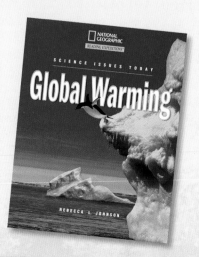

NATIONAL GEOGRAPHIC
READING EXPEDITIONS

SCIENCE ISSUES TODAY

Global Warming

REBECCA L. JOHNSON